Phillis Wheatley:
Poet of the Revolutionary Era

Molly Aloian

CRABTREE
Publishing Company
www.crabtreebooks.com

Understanding The American Revolution

Author: Molly Aloian

Publishing plan research and development:
 Sean Charlebois, Reagan Miller
 Crabtree Publishing Company

Editors: Leslie Jenkins, Janet Sweet, Phyllis Jelinek,
 Lynn Perrigo, Lynn Peppas

Proofreaders: Lisa Slone, Kelly McNiven

Editorial director: Kathy Middleton

Production coordinator: Shivi Sharma

Creative director: Amir Abbasi

Cover design: Samara Parent and Margaret Salter

Photo research: Nivisha Sinha

Maps: Paul Brinkdopke

Production coordinator and prepress technician: Samara Parent

Print coordinator: Katherine Berti

Written, developed, and produced by Planman Technologies

Cover: A picture of Phillis Wheatley from her famous book, *Poems on Various Subjects, Religious and Moral.*

Title page: (left) A portrayal of the British and citizens of Boston fighting at the Boston Massacre in 1770.
(right) A statue of Phillis Wheatley in Boston, Massachussetts

Photographs and Reproductions

Front Cover: © North Wind Picture Archives / Alamy (b) / Shutterstock (t); Title Page: Library of Congress; ©Randy Duchaine / Alamy / IndiaPicture; Table of Content: Architect of the Capitol; Library of Congress; Library of Congress; Library of Congress; Library of Congress; Introduction: Library of Congress; Chapter 1: Library of Congress; Chapter 2: Library of Congress; Chapter 3: Library of Congress; Chapter 4: Library of Congress; Page 4: ©The Art Gallery Collection / Alamy / IndiaPicture; Page 5: Architect of the Capitol; Page 8: Library of Congress; Page 10: Library of Congress; Page 11: ©Aurora Photos / Alamy / IndiaPicture (t); Library of Congress (b); Page 12: Library of Congress; Page 14: Library of Congress; Page 15: Library of Congress (t); ©Classic Image / Alamy / IndiaPicture (b); Page 16: ©Randy Duchaine / Alamy / IndiaPicture; Page 17: Library of Congress; Page 20: Library of Congress (t); Library of Congress (b); Page 23: Library of Congress; Page 24: Library of Congress; Page 25: Library of Congress (t); MPI / Archive Photos / Getty Images; Page 26: ©Aurora Photos / Alamy / IndiaPicture; Page 29: Everett/IndiaPicture (t); Library of Congress; Page 30: Library of Congress; Page 32: ©Randy Duchaine / Alamy / IndiaPicture; Page 33: Hulton Archive / Archive Photos / Getty Images; Page 34: Library of Congress; Page 35: Library of Congress (t); Library of Congress (b); Page 36: Library of Congress; Page 38: Library of Congress; Page 41: Library of Congress;
(t = top, b = bottom, l = left, c= center, r = right, bkgd = background, fgd = foreground)

Library and Archives Canada Cataloguing in Publication

Aloian, Molly
 Phillis Wheatley : poet of the revolutionary era / Molly Aloian.

(Understanding the American Revolution)
Includes bibliographical references and index.
Issued also in electronic format.
ISBN 978-0-7787-0803-2 (bound).--ISBN 978-0-7787-0814-8 (pbk.)

 1. Wheatley, Phillis, 1753-1784--Juvenile literature. 2. Poets, American--Colonial period, ca. 1600-1775--Biography--Juvenile literature. 3. African American women poets--Biography--Juvenile literature. 4. Women slaves--United States--Biography--Juvenile literature. I. Title. II. Series: Understanding the American Revolution (St. Catharines, Ont.)

PS866.W5Z54 2013   j811'.1   C2013-900242-1

Library of Congress Cataloging-in-Publication Data

CIP available at Library of Congress

Crabtree Publishing Company
www.crabtreebooks.com   1-800-387-7650

Printed in Canada/052014/TT20140331

Published in Canada
Crabtree Publishing
616 Welland Ave.
St. Catharines, Ontario
L2M 5V6

Published in the United States
Crabtree Publishing
PMB 59051
350 Fifth Avenue, 59th Floor
New York, New York 10118

Published in the United Kingdom
Crabtree Publishing
Maritime House
Basin Road North, Hove
BN41 1WR

Published in Australia
Crabtree Publishing
3 Charles Street
Coburg North
VIC 3058

TABLE *of* CONTENTS

Introduction

The American Revolution was one of the most important events in United States history. It was a war between thirteen British **colonies** in North America and their mother country, Great Britain. The war took place between 1775 and 1783. Many factors caused the war, and there were several major battles and a number of brave military leaders.

A cartoonist illustrates America's relationship with Great Britain in the 1700s.

Thirteen Colonies

When the American Revolution began in 1775, the United States was not divided into states as it is today. Instead of states, America was divided into 13 colonies. Colonies are areas of land that are owned by another country. Britain owned and controlled the American colonies.

British Rule

People from Europe, including many from Great Britain, sailed across the Atlantic Ocean to start new lives and claim land in the 13 colonies. The land held many valuable **natural resources**, including trees, rich soil, and plenty of wildlife. The British government tried to enforce laws and created taxes to increase its control over the colonies. Eventually, the colonists in America wanted **independence** from Britain. They did not want to be taxed or ruled by Britain any longer.

American Victory

During the American Revolution, the American troops managed to win important victories, which eventually led to an **alliance** with France. The eight years of fighting finally ended after the Battle of Yorktown in Virginia. The Revolutionary War ended in 1783 with an American victory. The colonies secured their independence from Great Britain, and the United States of America was born.

> *Yesterday, the greatest question was decided . . . and a greater [question], perhaps, never was or will be decided among Men. A resolution was passed without one dissenting colony, 'that these United Colonies are, and of right ought to be, free and independent states.'*
>
> —John Adams, leader of American independence and second president of the United States, 1776

Declaration of Independence

Hudson's Bay Company

Nova Scotia

Province of Quebec

Massachusetts

claimed by New York and New Hampshire

New Hampshire

Boston

Massachusetts

New York

Rhode Island
Connecticut

Pennsylvania

New York

New Jersey

Philadelphia

Baltimore

Delaware

Maryland

Indian Reserve

Virginia

Spanish Louisiana

North Carolina

ATLANTIC OCEAN

South Carolina

Georgia

Charleston

West Florida

East Florida

Gulf of Mexico

N E S W

	British Territory
	Thirteen Colonies (British)
	Spanish Territory
●	major city
– –	Proclamation Line of 1763*

0   125   250 miles
0   125   250 kilometers

*This line shows the farthest west British settlers were allowed to go. The rest of the land was reserved for Native Americans.

North America before the Revolutionary War

Hudson's Bay Company

claimed by New York
and New Hampshire

claimed by New York
and Massachusetts

Massachusetts

**New
York**

New Hampshire

Boston

Massachusetts

Rhode Island
Connecticut

Pennsylvania

New York

New Jersey

Philadelphia

Baltimore

Delaware

Maryland

Spanish
Louisiana

Virginia

claimed by
Virginia

claimed by
North Carolina

**North
Carolina**

claimed by
South Carolina

claimed by Georgia

**South
Carolina**

**ATLANTIC
OCEAN**

claimed by
United States
and Spain

Georgia

Charleston

N
W   E
S

0   125   250 miles
0   125   250 kilometers

Gulf of Mexico

Spanish
Florida

	British Territory
	United States
	Spanish Territory
	territory claimed by two states
	territory claimed by U.S. and Spain
•	major city

North America after the Revolutionary War

Snatched from Africa

Major Events

A young girl who would become Phillis Wheatley is snatched from her homeland and brought to the colonies.

A Terrible Journey

At the age of seven, a young African girl was seized by slave hunters and violently torn from her family. She was forced onto the slave ship *Phillis* and crammed into the storage space below the ship's deck, along with at least 200 other kidnapped Africans. For the next six to eight weeks, she became **cargo** on a terrifying journey from Africa all the way across the Atlantic Ocean to Boston, Massachusetts. She would never see her family or her homeland again.

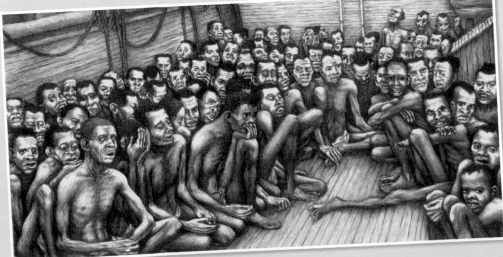

An artist imagines what conditions were like aboard a slave ship like the *Phillis*, which brought Phillis Wheatley to America.

A Miserable Arrival in America

When the *Phillis* arrived in Boston on July 11, 1761, the Africans on board were homesick, seasick, half starved, naked, ill, and terrified. Many had already died of hunger or thirst during the journey. Some died from diseases. Others were killed or threw themselves overboard out of pure terror. Despite their miserable conditions and suffering, an estimated four out of five Africans survived the slave ship journeys.

The Slave Trade Route

Like most slave trading ships during that time, the *Phillis* likely sailed up the west coast of Africa and headed across the Atlantic Ocean to the Caribbean. There, the strongest Africans on board were sold as slaves to do back-breaking work on sugarcane plantations. The *Phillis* would then sail to the Southern colonies. There, the slave traders sold more Africans to colonial plantation owners. These owners wanted slaves to work in their rice, tobacco, and cotton fields. Then the *Phillis* would sail north to its last stop in Boston.

Arriving in Boston

The last of the Africans on board the *Phillis* were transported to the shipping docks in Boston. These people were too young, too frail, or too sick to do rigorous labor in the West Indian and Southern colonies. The seven-year-old girl was among them, treated like livestock while waiting to be put up for sale as a slave.

Sold "for a Trifle"

Mrs. Susanna Wheatley was the wife of John Wheatley, a wealthy **tailor** and **merchant** in Boston. Wanting to purchase a house servant, Mrs. Wheatley went to the docks. There she saw "a slender, frail female child evidently suffering from a change of climate," nearly naked, and "about seven years old . . . from the circumstances of shedding [losing] her front teeth."

1762

By age 8, Phillis learns to speak, read, and write English

1763–1765

By age 11, Phillis masters difficult Bible passages and writes about the violence in Boston

1765

March 27
The British government imposes the Stamp Act on American colonists

1766–1767

By age 13, Phillis studies classical literature and translates it into sophisticated poems

1767

December
Phillis Wheatley's first poem is published in a newspaper

Aboard a Slave Ship

The conditions on board a slave ship were disgusting. Men, women, and children were chained tightly to plank beds or to each other with very little room to move. They were given hardly any food or water during the journey. Slaves could only relieve themselves in buckets. Sometimes, captains did not provide buckets, so slaves were forced to relieve themselves on the floor of the ship. Diseases were spread easily because of the poor hygiene and close quarters. Many people died from dehydration, **dysentery**, and **scurvy**.

Mrs. Wheatley bought the young girl "for a **trifle**." This amount was later estimated to be less than ten **pounds sterling**. The captain of the slave ship thought she was **terminally ill**, and he wanted to make at least a small profit before she died.

The Old State House in Boston, Massachusetts

A New Life

The seven-year-old slave boarded a carriage with her new owner. Mrs. Wheatley named the girl "Phillis" after the name of the ship that had brought her from Africa. As a servant, Phillis would have the same last name as her owner.

In the Heart of American History

Phillis's new home, the Wheatley mansion, was located on the corner of King Street and Mackerel Lane, just a few blocks from the Old State House in Boston. Both the Stamp Act riots of 1765 and the Boston Massacre of 1770 took place down the street from the Wheatleys' front door. Living in the midst of "history in the making" became a tremendous influence on the poetry that Phillis later wrote.

The Old State House: Where History Happened

The Old State House was the center of Boston's **civic** life and the scene of some of the most dramatic events leading up to the American Revolution. Within its walls, John Hancock, John Adams, and other **Patriot** leaders debated the future of the American colonies. Just outside the building, five men were among the first casualties of the battle for independence, in what would later be known as the Boston Massacre. From the building's balcony, the Declaration of Independence was proclaimed in 1776 to the citizens of Boston.

Memories of Home

Phillis Wheatley's exact date of birth and her African name remain unknown. It's believed that Phillis was kidnapped from Senegal in Western Africa, where she was one of the **Muslim** people known as the Fula. Traditionally, the Fula were **nomadic** people who kept herds of cattle, goats, and sheep.

One of Phillis's only memories from her home in Africa was of her mother. She remembered her mother pouring water in a ritual to the sun as it rose. The rising sun is mentioned in many of Phillis's poems.

Slaves in Boston

Unlike slaves who worked on plantations in the Southern colonies, many slaves in the Northern colonies—where there were more cities than farms—worked as house servants. Others did skilled labor to support the local trades, such as carpentry, shipbuilding, sail making, printing, blacksmithing, and weaving. By the late 1700s, nearly 20 percent of the 13 colonies' population was of African **descent**. Almost all of these people were slaves.

Slaves had no rights and were not paid for the work that they did. In 1762, the year after Phillis arrived in Boston, the city had over 15,500 people. About 1,000 were Africans or African Americans. Of these, only 18 were free blacks. No black children "could be counted among the more than 800 students enrolled in the city's [five] schools."

> *Slavery is a bitter pill, . . . [O]ur day's work was never done. . . . I was often brought to weep between the porch and the altar.*
>
> —Richard Allen, 1760–1831, former slave during the 1700s

This Fula boy cares for goats in the same way that his ancestors once did.

This illustration shows slaves working in a cotton field in the 1700s.

What Do You Know!

ASTHMA

Phillis was not very strong and she was often sick. Historians believe she suffered from **chronic asthma**. Her frail condition and pleasant good looks may have led to her receiving special treatment from the Wheatleys.

Asthma is a chronic **respiratory** disease that narrows the airway to the lungs. It makes breathing difficult and causes **inflammation** of the airway. Smoke, pollution, cold air, and humidity can trigger asthma, which can make sleeping difficult. Common symptoms of asthma are coughing, **wheezing**, chest tightness, and shortness of breath.

> *To Be Sold; A Parcel of likely Negroes, imported from Africa, cheap for cash, or short credit; Enquire of John Avery.*
>
> —Boston Gazette, July 29, 1761

A Prominent Family

John Wheatley made a good living as a tailor. He and his wife had a large home. He also owned a store, several warehouses, and a merchant **schooner** called the *London Packet*. John and Susanna owned a number of slaves, but their slaves were getting old and weak, and Susanna wanted a young girl to help with household chores.

The Wheatley Family

Susanna and John Wheatley had two children—twins Nathaniel and Mary. Phillis arrived when she was seven years old. Nathaniel and Mary were 18 year olds.

The Wheatleys treated their slaves better than many other families in Boston. Mrs. Wheatley was especially fond of Phillis. According to one of her relatives, Mrs. Wheatley liked "the modest demeanor and the interesting features of the little stranger." As a result, Phillis was not treated like an ordinary slave. She was given special privileges that were practically unheard of during that time.

A drawing of a slave auction.

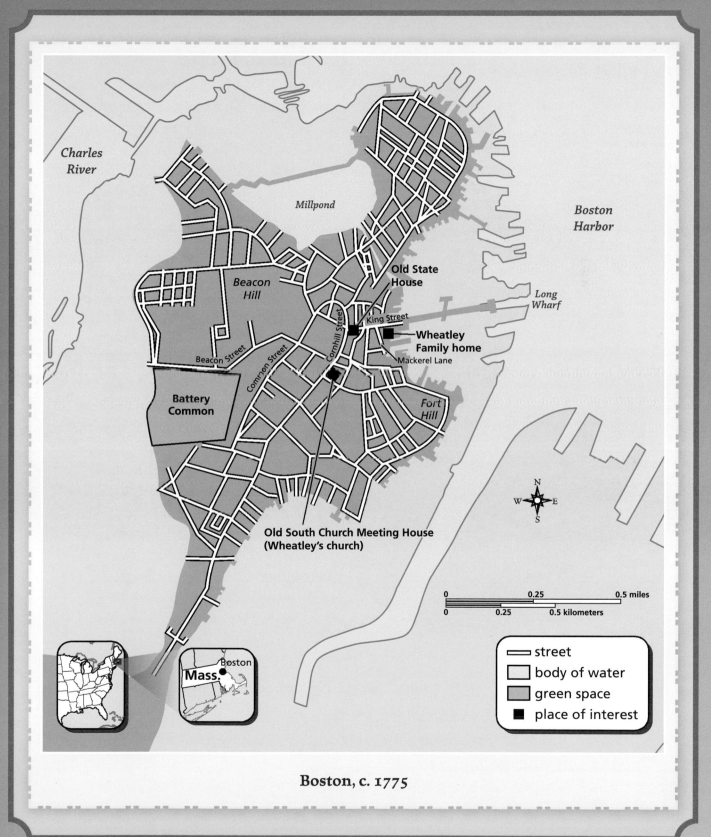

Charles
River

Millpond

Boston
Harbor

Beacon
Hill

Old State
House

Long
Wharf

King Street

Cornhill Street

Wheatley
Family home

Beacon Street

Mackerel Lane

Common Street

Battery
Common

Fort
Hill

Old South Church Meeting House
(Wheatley's church)

0   0.25   0.5 miles
0   0.25   0.5 kilometers

Boston

Mass.

▭ street
▢ body of water
▨ green space
■ place of interest

Boston, c. 1775

🐚 **What Do You Think?**

Why do you think Mary Wheatley knew how to teach Phillis to read Greek and Latin?

Learning to Read and Write

The Wheatleys noticed right away that Phillis was intelligent, eager, and quick to learn new things. Their 18-year-old daughter, Mary Wheatley, wanted to be a teacher, so she and her mother started teaching Phillis. Mrs. Wheatley did not entirely excuse Phillis from her **domestic** duties, but she allowed Mary to teach Phillis how to read and write. Within a few months—by the time she was eight—Phillis learned how to read and speak English. It was very unusual for a slave to be able to read and write, and the Wheatleys liked to show Phillis off to other prominent families in the Boston area.

Love of Learning

Phillis's English continued to improve. She quickly understood the most difficult passages in the Bible. Mary taught Phillis how to read ancient Greek and Latin and encouraged her to study ancient writers in those languages. Phillis loved what she read. She was constantly eager to learn more. The Wheatleys owned many books and, before long, Phillis had read them all.

The young Phillis Wheatley

> *She [Phillis] was a pretty smart sprightly child. They grew very fond of her and treated her as well as if their own . . . . She never was looked on as a slave. She could work handsome [sew and do needlework skillfully] and read and write well for that day.*
>
> —Hannah Mather Crocker (1752–1829), American essayist and one of the first advocates of women's rights in America

Inspiring Poets

When she was 12 years old, Phillis began studying the poetry of the English writer Alexander Pope. Pope is famous for his use of the **heroic couplet**. He is also known for his **translations** of the long story-like poems written by the ancient Greek writer Homer. Phillis enjoyed Pope's translations of Homer's writing. In fact, she learned about the rhythm of poetry from reading Pope. She also began writing her own translations of Homer's work.

A Surprise to Scholars

Phillis also found the works of an ancient Roman writer named Ovid. Within a few years, she was reading his stories in Latin and translating them into heroic couplets in English. Many scholars in Boston were surprised by, and impressed with, Phillis's abilities. They had never known a slave to be able to translate ancient Greek and Latin classics into English.

> *Unblemish'd let me live,*
> *or die unknown;*
> *O grant an honest fame,*
> *or grant me none!*
>
> —Alexander Pope,
> "The Temple of Fame," 1715

People at the Time

Alexander Pope

Alexander Pope was one of the most famous British poets of the early 1700s. Phillis Wheatley may have admired Pope, in part, because they had a lot in common:

- He showed his intelligence at a very young age;
- He educated himself through extensive reading and studying;
- As a Catholic, he was an outsider who expressed his views through poetry.

Ovid was a Roman poet whose most famous work is "Metamorphoses."

Still a Slave

Mrs. Wheatley made sure Phillis had a quill, ink, paper, and a candle so that she could write when she wanted, even at night. Unlike other slaves, Phillis had her own room in the attic. Her room had heating, and she was given candles to use for light. These privileges were unusual for a slave. Although the Wheatleys treated Phillis very well, they never forgot that she was a slave. She was still expected to help with household chores.

First Letter

Phillis often saw Mrs. Wheatley writing letters to her friends, so Phillis began to write letters, too. She wrote one of her first letters to Mrs. Wheatley's friend, Reverend Samson Occom. Reverend Occom was a traveling Native American minister who preached for a time in England.

Soon after, Phillis wrote her very first poem called "On the Death of the Rev. Dr. Sewell [**sic**] when sick, 1765." Reverend Sewall was a pastor at the church that the Wheatleys and Phillis attended. Reverend Sewall was very sick when Phillis wrote the poem. The poem was an **elegy**. Phillis had read elegies written by Alexander Pope when she was younger.

ᕓ Quill Pen

From the 1700s through the 1800s, people wrote with quill pens, also called dip pens, which were made from sturdy reeds or feathers. Writing with a quill pen was not easy and required a lot of practice.

The Boston Women's Memorial depicts Phillis Wheatley with a quill in her hand.

A Story Inspires

In the fall of 1767, John Wheatley invited two gentlemen, Mr. Hussey and Mr. Coffin, to dinner. During the meal, the men told John about being caught in a terrible storm off Cape Cod. Phillis overheard the story and was inspired to write a poem about the gentlemen and their narrow escape.

Mrs. Wheatley read the poem and thought it was good enough to be printed in a newspaper. Phillis's first poem, "On Messrs [Misters] Hussey and Coffin" was published in the *Newport Mercury* newspaper on December 21, 1767. Phillis was just 14 years old.

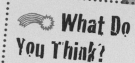

What Do You Think?

Why would a story about ocean danger and risking lives inspire Phillis to write a poem about it?

A storm on the ocean, like this one shown tossing a boat, inspired Phillis's first published poem.

 What Do You Know!

ELEGY
An elegy is a poem written in response to a person's death. Poets in ancient Greece developed this poetic form, which traditionally expresses three stages of loss. The first stage is the lament, or expression of grief and sorrow. The second stage expresses praise and admiration—sometimes **idealized**—for the dead person. The third stage offers **consolation** and comfort to those who will miss the person.

Becoming a Well-known Poet

During the next six years, Phillis Wheatley and her poetry became widely known in colonial New England. Her poetry covered religion, freedom, and significant events leading up to the American Revolution. She was still a slave, but her talent for writing was making an impact in the literary world.

A Life Apart

Phillis was the property of the Wheatleys, but she had privileges that other slaves rarely had, such as a heated room, access to books, and most importantly, an education. In general, her role was unclear in the family and in society. She was not allowed to eat at the table with the Wheatleys, yet the other slaves viewed her as an outsider, too. She was cut off from any normal contact that would help her identify with black groups or with white groups.

As a result, Phillis did not belong to either group. Literary experts believe her poems were popular because they reflected the events during this revolutionary time in America's history from an outsider's view.

The Wheatleys continued to give Phillis special attention for her talents. They showed her off to their many wealthy friends. Guests came to the Wheatleys to visit this "lovely and brilliant conversationalist."

Major Events

1768-69
Phillis becomes well- known for writing poems celebrating America, freedom, and religion

1770
Phillis's poem honoring an important British preacher makes her famous

March 5
The Boston Massacre occurs down the street from the Wheatley mansion

What Do You Think?
How did being outside the worlds of both black and white people give Phillis an unusual view of people and events at that time?

Inspiration

In the fall of 1770, when Phillis was just 16, she wrote a poem about a British preacher named Reverend George Whitefield. Phillis admired Reverend Whitefield. He was one of the most exciting speakers in all of the colonies. When he died suddenly on September 30, 1770, Phillis quickly composed a poem praising him. She called the poem "An Elegiac Poem, On the Death of that Celebrated Divine, and Eminent Servant of Jesus Christ, the Late Reverend, and Pious George Whitefield." Phillis gained a wide readership in both Britain and America for this poem.

For Reverend Whitefield

Phillis's elegy for Reverend Whitefield is divided into three sections. For example, in the first section of the poem—the **lament**—she compares the sadness of Whitefield's death to the unhappiness of losing sunlight:

> *Unhappy we, the setting Sun deplore!*
> *Which once was splendid, but it shines no more;*

In the second section, she expresses her admiration for Whitefield's message that all Americans, regardless of race or class, are in need of **salvation**:

> *He pray'd that grace in every heart might dwell:*
> *He long'd to see America excel;*
> *He charg'd its youth to let the grace divine*
> *Arise, and in their future actions shine;*

In the third section, Phillis offers comfort to his admirers who are now left behind as "orphans" by suggesting they think of him in "yon azure skies," or heaven:

> *New-England sure, doth feel the ORPHAN's smart; . . .*
> *Then let us view him in yon azure skies:*
> *Let every mind with this lov'd object rise.*

1772

October
At age 18, Phillis and her owner decide to publish a book of Phillis's poems

November 14
A powerful group of Boston's leaders test Phillis's intelligence and confirms that her work is her own

1773

May 8
Phillis travels to England; she is welcomed as a literary celebrity in London

May 10
Britain imposes the Tea Act on the colonies

September
Mrs. Wheatley becomes ill; Phillis's book of poetry, *Poems on Various Subjects, Religious and Moral* is published

December 3
The Boston Tea Party

The Reverend
George Whitefield

Religious Inspiration

Phillis was deeply influenced by the British Reverend George Whitefield. He had a powerful voice and tremendous energy, and he had preached in a dramatic style that crowds loved. His sermons had captured the spellbound attention of his huge audiences.

Whitefield had toured the colonies seven times between the 1760s and the 1770s, and had been popular on both sides of the Atlantic. For both Americans and the British, his sermons were the single shared religious experience that connected them to each other. His message of turning away from a life of sin through **personal salvation** inspired Phillis to want to be baptized. Slaves were not usually baptized in church. But on August 18, 1771, Phillis was baptized at Boston's Old South Meeting House Church. This was the church she had attended with the Wheatleys since arriving in America.

Making Progress

The speed with which Phillis wrote her elegy for Reverend Whitefield and the quality of the poem's language showed the progress she had made as a poet. The poem was published as a **broadside**—a large poster displayed in public—in New York, Philadelphia, Rhode Island, and Boston, and also in London, England.

Old South Church

Promoting Her Poetry

Phillis's name was now spreading beyond Boston. She quickly wrote several other poems on the deaths of prominent English and colonial leaders and the members of their families. In one poem about the death of a child, Phillis wrote, "Freed from a world of sin, and snares, and pain, why would you wish your daughter back again?" Her writing gave comfort to those who had lost loved ones and was often printed in colonial newspapers.

Mrs. Wheatley supported Phillis's writing by introducing her to powerful people who would promote her work. Phillis often entertained the Wheatleys' guests with her poetry and was invited to other homes to read her poetry.

Possibly a Book

By 1772, Phillis's fame had spread beyond the colonies, and she had written enough poems to fill a book. Mrs. Wheatley believed Phillis's poems should be published. However, before a book could be published a certain amount of people had to **subscribe** to it. This meant they had to agree to buy the book when it was printed. It would guarantee that the printer would be paid for his work. Although some people in Boston subscribed, the number of subscribers needed to publish the book could not be found.

AMERICAN VIEWS OF AFRICANS

Most colonists in Boston could not believe that an African slave—much less a girl—was intelligent enough to write a poem by herself. Influential leaders of that time believed that Africans and other dark-skinned people belonged to a separate, inferior category of humans. As a result, most Americans and Europeans believed only white people were considered intelligent and capable of writing a literary work.

> "
> *I am apt to suspect the negroes and . . . all other species of men to be naturally inferior to the whites. There never was a civilized nation of any other complexion than white.*
>
> —18th-century philosopher David Hume
> "

American colonists associated African slaves with manual labor. Never before had an African slave demonstrated the ability to create imaginative literature. Not all colonists were able to read and write themselves. They had to depend on people with reading knowledge to keep them informed of news and laws. The idea that an African slave could be among those people was beyond belief.

Demanding Proof

Both Mrs. Wheatley and Phillis thought they might have a better chance of getting the book published in Great Britain. Mrs. Wheatley was friends with Selina Hastings, the Countess of Huntingdon, a wealthy and **influential** woman in London. Phillis wrote to the countess to ask for her support. She also wrote to Archibald Bell, an important bookseller and printer in London. Bell thought is was highly unlikely that a slave in the colonies could write poetry without help. He demanded proof that Phillis had written the poems herself.

On October 8, 1772, Susanna Wheatley gathered 18 of Boston's most important and educated citizens to question Phillis. Their purpose was to decide if she was truly the author of the poems she claimed to have written.

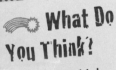

What Do You Think?

Why do you think Phillis agreed to be questioned about her abilities as a poet?

Deciding Her Fate

This group of powerful and privileged men included six **Loyalists** and several Patriot leaders. Nearly all of them were Harvard graduates, and most of them owned slaves. One of them had been a slave dealer, and another did not believe in allowing "women and girls; yea Negroes. . . to do the business of preachers [like Reverend Whitefield]."

High Stakes that Affect Slavery

If Phillis passed their test, then it would prove that Africans were intelligent human beings and should be liberated from slavery. If Phillis failed to show that she could write poetry on her own, then she—and all Africans who claimed they could write—would be viewed as a parrot that simply repeated what others told it. As Harvard Professor Henry Louis Gates, Jr, wrote, "This trial was . . . one of the most dramatic contests over literacy, authenticity, and humanity in the history of race relations in this country."

Passing the Test

Phillis, a shy 18-year-old African slave, stood before this group of several of the finest minds in all of colonial America and amazed them with her pure, unassisted intelligence. Thomas Woolbridge was among the group of men examining Phillis's abilities. He later wrote, "I . . . . found by conversing [talking] with the African, that she was no imposter [fake] . . . . I was astonished, and could hardly believe my own Eyes. I was present when she wrote, and can attest that it is her own production."

Despite this confirmation of Phillis's abilities, some Boston colonists remained skeptical, simply because she was an African slave.

WHO WERE THE 18 MEN? The 18 men questioning Phillis were all men of wealth, learning, and **stature**. They were statesmen, scholars, clergy, poets, merchants, and lawyers. Here are some of their names and positions:

- His Excellency Thomas Hutchinson, Governor of the Colony
- The Honorable Andrew Oliver, Lieutenant Governor
- The Honorable Thomas Hubbard, a deacon at Old South Church
- The Honorable James Bowdoin, a published poet, friend of Benjamin Franklin, and future governor of Massachusetts
- Mr. John Hancock, Patriot leader, signer of the Declaration of Independence, and future governor of Massachusetts
- Mr. Joseph Green, merchant and man of letters who owned one of Boston's largest libraries
- The Reverend Charles Chauncy, pastor of the First Church of Boston
- The Reverend Andrew Elliot, pastor of New North Church in Boston
- The Reverend Samuel Cooper, minister of Brattle Street Church
- The Reverend John Moorhead, pastor of the Scotch Presbyterian Church.
- Mr. John Wheatley, Phillis's master and Boston merchant and businessman

People at the Time

John Hancock

John Hancock was one of the wealthiest men in the colonies during the 1770s. He later served as president of the Second Continental Congress and was also the governor of Massachusetts. He was the first person to sign the Declaration of Independence and is remembered for his large and stylish signature on the document. Today, the name "John Hancock" is often used as a synonym, or word that means the same thing, for the word "signature."

Finding a Patron

Mrs. Wheatley and the Countess of Huntingdon admired many of the same ministers. In fact, Reverend George Whitefield had been the countess's private clergyman. The countess was wealthy and powerful, and she donated plenty of money to religious and anti-slavery causes. She instructed Archibald Bell, the printer who had demanded proof of Phillis's claims, to begin working with Phillis on her book. Against the greatest odds, the first book of poetry written by an African slave woman would be published.

Humble Appreciation

Phillis dedicated the book to the countess even though the two women had never met. The dedication said, "To the Right Honorable, the Countess of Huntingdon, the following poems are most respectfully inscribed by her much obliged, very humble, and devoted servant, Phillis Wheatley." Phillis also hoped that under the countess's **patronage**, her "feeble efforts will be shielded from the severe trials of uppity Criticism."

Selina Hastings, the Countess of Huntingdon

Celebrated in London

Early in 1773, Phillis's asthma made her very sick, and Mrs. Wheatley became worried. The Wheatleys decided to send Phillis, by then about 20 years old, to London so she could avoid the harsh Boston winter. In early May, she traveled with Nathaniel Wheatley, who was going to London on business.

Phillis had become famous as the African slave poetess, and she was welcomed by many important dignitaries in London. Among them were the anti-slavery **abolitionist** Granville Sharpe, poet Baron George Lyttleton, and American Patriot Benjamin Franklin, who was in London as a **spokesperson** for the American colonies.

Abolition

The anti-slavery movement in colonial America was a small group that was considered quite **radical**. English reformers took the lead in protesting against slavery. They were joined by Americans with varied motives. Religious societies, especially in the Northern colonies, stressed the moral evil of the trade. Free blacks saw the end of the slave trade as a first step toward overall freedom in general. By the mid-1770s, abolitionist organizations had begun to form in some of the northern states.

> *Without continual growth and progress, such words as improvement, achievement, and success have no meaning.*
>
> —Benjamin Franklin

People at the Time

Benjamin Franklin

Benjamin Franklin was a famous writer, inventor, statesman, and philosopher and is one of the Founding Fathers of the United States. During the American Revolution, he helped write important documents, including the Declaration of Independence.

He supported Phillis and her writing. Like most people of his period, Franklin initially believed that African slaves and their offspring were inferior to white Europeans and that they could not be educated. He began to question his beliefs when he visited a school where young African children were being taught. In 1763, he wrote a letter to an English friend where he stated, "I . . . have . . . a higher opinion of the natural capacities of the black race, than I had ever before entertained. . . . [They are] in every respect equal to that of white children."

Franklin was convinced that slavery and the slave trade should be eliminated. In his position of president of the Pennsylvania anti-slavery society, Franklin addressed the education of former slaves.

A sketch based on a medallion of the Pennsylvania **Abolition** Society.

A Trip Cut Short

Phillis's trip was cut short. She received word at the end of the summer that Mrs. Wheatley had become seriously ill. Phillis cancelled a planned visit with King George III and the royal family to return to Boston to care for her.

Finally Published

While Phillis was crossing the Atlantic Ocean returning to Boston, Archibald Bell distributed the first edition of her book of poems. The book, titled *Poems on Various Subjects, Religious and Moral*, contained 28 poems. At last, her book of poetry was published. At just 20 years of age, she was the first African-American slave ever to publish a book of poems.

The cover of *Poems on Various Subjects, Religious and Moral*, which was published in 1773.

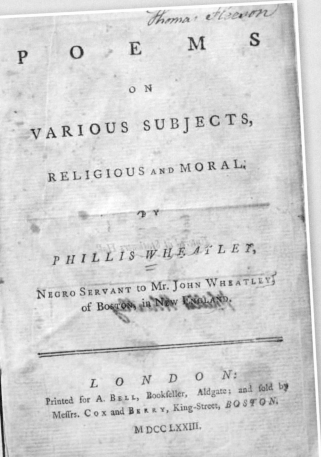

Prominent Boston Endorsement

A special statement from the 18 important Boston citizens, as well as testimony from John Wheatley, accompanied the *Poems on Various Subjects, Religious and Moral.* The statement read:

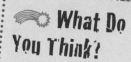
What Do You Think?

Why would the 18 prominent Boston men who questioned Phillis be surprised that she proved her abilities as a poet?

> *Phillis was brought from Africa to America, in the Year 1761, between Seven and Eight Years of Age. Without any Assistance from School Education, and by only what she was taught in the Family, she, in sixteen Months Time from her Arrival, attained the English Language, to which she was an utter Stranger before, to such a Degree, as to read any, the most difficult Parts of the Sacred Writings, to the great Astonishment of all who heard her. As to her WRITING, her own Curiosity led her to it; and this she learnt in so short a Time, that in the Year 1765, she wrote a LETTER to the Rev. Mr. Occom, the Indian Minister, while in England. She has a great Inclination to learn the Latin Tongue, and has made some Progress in it. This Relation is given by her Master who bought her, and with whom she now lives.*

Revolutionary Writings

Major Events

1770

Phillis writes a poem about the death of a boy who is accidentally shot

March 5
Boston Massacre

1773

Phillis Wheatley is set free; she is no longer a slave

1775

Phillis writes "To His Excellency, General Washington"

Phillis Wheatley lived and wrote during a **tumultuous** time in American history. She was not considered a citizen herself, but she watched citizens resist British rule. She witnessed the events of the Revolutionary War just down the street from where she lived.

The Desire for Independence

As a slave, Phillis understood the desire to be free. As an outsider, she had an **untainted** view of events. As a religious woman, she had a humble desire for change through goodness. As a respected and gifted poet, she had the language and means to show the troubling issues of the Revolutionary War to the world.

The Stamp Act

In 1765, the British government needed money to pay off old war debts. So on March 22, it decided to make American colonists pay a new tax in order to raise the money. American colonists were required to pay taxes on every piece of printed paper they used, including legal papers, newspapers, licenses, and even playing cards. This was called the Stamp Act.

America Protests

Many colonists were outraged by the Stamp Act. On the day that the tax took effect, shops were closed and the colonists protested. Some colonists refused to pay the tax and ran tax collectors out of town. When King George III decided to end the Stamp Act in 1766, American colonists celebrated.

Stamps like these were attached to documents to show the Stamp Act tax had been paid.

Poetic Comment on the Stamp Act

After King George III brought an end to the Stamp Act, Phillis wrote a poem called "To the King's Most Excellent Majesty." The poem recalls the event and praises the king's decision to end the Stamp Act.

In the poem, she praises King George III:

> *YOUR subjects hope. . .*
> *The crown upon your brows may flourish long*

She also points out the importance of listening to the colonists' desire for independence:

> *Midst the remembrance of thy favours past,*
> *The meanest peasants most admire the last*

Virginia representatives, including Patrick Henry, debate the colonies' relationship with Great Britain.

 What Do You Know!

THE STAMP ACT

Taxation stamps were commonly used in Britain in colonial times. Sir George Grenville thought it would be a good idea to use stamps to tax goods in America as well. Grenville and the British Parliament did not expect the outcry against the Stamp Act in the colonies. Colonists thought it was unfair to pay a stamp tax since they had no representation in Parliament. The Stamp Act was **repealed** in 1766, but Parliament passed the Declaratory Act the same year. This act said that Parliament had the right to tax the colonies in any way it desired.

Another Poem Protesting the Stamp Act

Phillis wrote another poem called "On America, 1768," this time reflecting the colonists' outrage over the Stamp Act. The poem describes the history of New England, from its founding to the period of tension between Britain and America.

In the following lines, the poem urges Britain ("a certain lady") to improve its relations with America ("an only son") before it is too late. The poem suggests that, otherwise, America will continue to grow strong enough to overpower Britain.

> *A certain lady had an only son*
> *He grew up daily virtuous as he grew*
> *Fearing his Strength which she undoubtedly knew*
> *She laid some taxes on her darling son . . .*
> *And would have laid another act there on.*
> *'Amend your manners I'll the task remove'*
> *Was said with seeming Sympathy and Love*
> *By many Scourges she his goodness try'd*
> *Untill at length the Best of Infants cry'd.*
> *He wept, Brittania turn'd a senseless ear. . .*
>
> —Phillis Wheatley

People at the Time

George Washington

George Washington was the leader of the colonial Continental Army during the Revolutionary War. He was appointed commander in chief of the army in 1775. He had fought bravely in the French and Indian Wars, and people admired his strength and courage. After the Revolutionary War, he became the first president of the United States. The capital—Washington, D.C.—is named after him.

> *My first wish is to see this plague to mankind [war] banished from off the earth.*
>
> —George Washington July 25, 1785

Freedom from Slavery

Phillis kept writing about what she saw around her. She continued to witness the violence in the streets of Boston leading up to the Revolutionary War and the colonists' struggle for freedom. Her own freedom came in 1773, when the Wheatleys released her from slavery. They were likely urged to do so by Phillis's influential abolitionist friends in London.

> "
> *Since my return to America, my Master has at the desire of my friends in England given me my freedom.*
>
> —Phillis Wheatley, in a letter dated October 18, 1773
> "

Writing in Support of Abolition

Phillis knew that freedom was on the minds of the people in Boston, as well as those in London. Slavery and America's struggle for freedom are topics that overlap in her poem "To the Right and Honorable William, Earl of Dartmouth." She became friends with the Earl of Dartmouth, who was a patron of abolitionists, on her trip to London in 1773. Phillis wrote this poem to share four important points with him in her message about slavery.

First, she thanks him for what he has done on behalf of abolition. As a result of his efforts, slaves ("Each soul") can gratefully see the possibility ("behold the silken reins") of freedom:

> *Elate with hope her race no longer mourns,*
> *Each soul expands, each grateful bosom burns,*
> *While in thine hand with pleasure we behold*
> *The silken reins, and Freedom's charms unfold*

Second, she anticipates the day when slavery is outlawed in America:

> *No longer shalt thou [slaves in America] dread the iron chain,*
> *Which wanton Tyranny with lawless hand*
> *Had made, and with it meant t' enslave the land.*

The Earl of Dartmouth had been appointed secretary of state for the colonies and president of the Board of Trade and Foreign Plantations in August of 1772. He held the position until November of 1775, and was considered a friend to those who opposed slavery.

Phillis considered the Earl of Dartmouth a friend of the colonists, and her poem expresses the hopes that she and many other colonists had for freedom in America. In her poem, she refers to the "cruel fate" of being kidnapped from Africa and the sorrow this must have caused her family. Phillis realized the value of liberty and wanted to spare others the pain she suffered as an enslaved individual.

Third, she emphasizes—from her own personal experience—how cruel slavery is. In this excerpt, she describes the loss of her life in Africa:

> *I, young in life, by seeming cruel fate*
> *Was snatch'd from Afric's fancy'd happy seat* [from her
>   homeland in Africa]

. . . and the terrible pain and sadness her parents must have felt when she was kidnapped from them:

> *What pangs excruciating must molest,*
> *What sorrows labour in my parent's breast?*

Last, she appeals to the Earl of Dartmouth to continue working for the abolition of slavery:

> *For favours past, great Sir, our thanks are due,*
> *And thee we ask thy favors to renew,*

Phillis Wheatley as a young woman.

The Contradiction between Colonists and Slaves

In 1765, when Phillis Wheatley was about 11 years old, she wrote a letter to Reverend Samson Occum, a Mohegan Indian, a preacher, and a poet. Despite the difference in their ages (Occum was 20 years older), her letter led to a friendship with Occum.

On February 11, 1774, Wheatley wrote Occum again, to agree with an argument he wrote criticizing Christian preachers who kept slaves. Phillis generally avoided strong language in addressing slavery. Her strongest anti-slavery statement is contained in this letter.

Only a few months earlier, she had been welcomed by important British dignitaries, who understood the importance of abolition. Now she was back in Boston, caring for her seriously ill mistress and witnessing Boston's reaction to British **oppression**.

In her letter, Phillis wrote that she was "greatly satisfied with your Reasons representing [slavery]." She implored God to convince all Americans in favor of slavery of the "strange Absurdity of their Conduct whose Words and Actions are so [totally] opposite."

She pointed out the **contradiction** between the colonists' demands for freedom from Britain and their determination to uphold slavery.

People at the Time

Samson Occum

Samson Occum was born in 1723 to Joshua Tomocham and his wife Sarah, a Mohegan Native American. At age 16, Occum became interested in missionaries and began to study English. He converted to Christianity in 1740. He became an ordained minister in 1759 and worked with Reverend George Whitefield. Occum spent two years in Britain raising money for a school in New Hampshire, which is now Dartmouth college. He spent the rest of his life as a missionary to other Native Americans. He and his wife Mary Fowler had 10 children. Occum died in 1792.

The Reverend Samson Occum

SAMSON OCCOM.

The Boston Massacre

Phillis also wrote about another violent incident that took place on March 5, 1770, between colonists and British soldiers. Known today as the Boston Massacre, the event took the lives of five men including Crispus Attucks, a **fugitive** slave who had run away from his master 20 years earlier.

Writing about Violence in Boston

Phillis wrote about the death of Christopher Snider, an 11-year-old boy who was shot during a skirmish in Boston. She also wrote about the events of the Boston Massacre in a poem called "On the Affray in King Street, on the Evening of the 5th of March." Phillis was living with the Wheatleys in their mansion just down the street from where the violence occurred, so she was probably an eyewitness to that tragic event.

An engraving of the Boston Massacre by Paul Revere, which was published in 1770.

Celebrations of America

True to her religious upbringing, Phillis was proud of what was good and right about America. Many of her poems focused on the theme of celebrating America. She was hopeful that slave owners would eventually support the idea of equality and liberty for all people, including Africans.

Phillis's most famous **patriotic** poem was called "To His Excellency, General Washington." She wrote the poem in 1775 to celebrate the accomplishments of George Washington and to show her **allegiance** to the revolutionary cause.

By April of 1775, the Revolutionary War between Britain and the American colonies had officially begun, and George Washington had been appointed commander in chief of the colonial troops. Phillis liked General Washington's position against the British. She sent him her poem along with a personal letter on October 26, 1775.

General George Washington

The Battle of Lexington: War Begins

Sir,

I have taken the freedom to address your Excellency in the enclosed poem, and entreat your acceptance, though I am not insensible of its inaccuracies. Your being appointed by the Grand Continental Congress to be Generalissimo of the armies of North America, together with the fame of your virtues, excite sensations not easy to suppress. Your generosity, therefore, I presume, will pardon the attempt. Wishing your Excellency all possible success in the great cause you are so generously engaged in. I am,

Your Excellency's most obedient humble servant,
Phillis Wheatley. Providence, Oct 26, 1775.

A Poem of Admiration

There are three messages in Phillis's poem, "To His Excellency, General Washington." First, she describes America's growing power, referring to America as both "Columbia" and "The Goddess." Then she praises Washington's military accomplishments "in peace and honors." Last she **rebuffs** anyone who dares to challenge "The land of freedom's heaven-defended race!" and wishes Washington's army great success.

A symbolic painting of America's growing power.

Freedom and War

After the American Revolution, Phillis Wheatley continued to write poetry. Sadly, she would only live a few more years of difficulty and hardship.

Revolutionary Changes

The Revolutionary War drastically changed Phillis's life. She continued to write poems and letters in hopes of publishing another book. In spite of her tremendous fame, Americans did not support her efforts. Colonists were dealing with the hardships of the war, and many still carried doubts about African slaves. During that time, her **benefactors** died or moved away, leaving her alone to fend for herself. The final years of her life were full of suffering and hardship. Once respected and celebrated—as a slave—for her talent and brilliance, Phillis Wheatley died alone—as a free woman—in **wretched** poverty and misery.

A Great Loss

Phillis tried her best to nurse Mrs. Wheatley back to health, but Susanna died in March of 1774 at the age of 65. Phillis was **devastated**. In a letter to her friend, Obour Tanner, Phillis wrote, "Let us imagine the loss of a parent, sister or brother, the tenderness of all these were united in her. I was a poor little outcast & stranger when she took me in: not only into the house, but I presently became a sharer in her most tender affections."

Major Events

1774

January
At age 20, Phillis tries to publish a second book

March 3
Mrs. Wheatley dies

March
Britain imposes the Intolerable Acts on America

September 5
The Continental Congress meets for the first time

1775

April 19
Revolutionary War begins

June 15
George Washington becomes Commander in chief

October 26
At age 21, Phillis writes a patriotic poem honoring George Washington

Major Events

1776

March 17
At age 22, Phillis meets with George Washington in Cambridge

1778

Mr. Wheatley and his children move away; at age 24 Phillis marries John Peters, a free African American

1779-1783

By age 29, Phillis gives birth to two children, who both die as toddlers; her husband often abandons her; Phillis lives in poverty unable to publish her second book

1781

October 19
British troops surrender to the Continental Army at Yorktown, Virginia

1783

September 3
The Treaty of Paris is signed, officially ending the Revolutionary War

1784

December 5
At age 30, Phillis dies alone, sick and poor, next to her dying baby; her infant son dies a few hours later

The British Leave Boston

Under General Washington's leadership, the British could not take over Boston. The Continental Army had gathered troops and ammunition from all the other colonies. The British realized that they were defeated in Boston. On March 17, 1776, British soldiers left Massachusetts, but the war kept on raging between Britain and the remaining American colonies.

ADMIRATION FOR WASHINGTON In 1775, Phillis sent a patriotic poem titled "To His Excellency General Washington" as a gift to Washington. She admired his leadership and abilities and wished him "all possible success in the great cause you are so generously engaged in."

Washington also admired her "poetical talents with great respect," and invited Phillis to visit him at his military headquarters in Cambridge, outside Boston. In March of 1776, Phillis accepted Washington's invitation to meet, and she visited with him on the day that the British soldiers left Massachusetts.

General George Washington

Struggling to Survive

Phillis struggled physically and emotionally during the harsh war years after Mrs. Wheatley's death. She was often sick from her chronic asthma. The constant political upsets and violent fights occurring in Boston weighed heavily on her emotions.

Then John Wheatley moved away from Boston to be with relatives. Since Mary Wheatley lived with her husband in Rhode Island and Nathaniel Wheatley lived with his wife in London, this left Phillis homeless. At the age of 24, she was entirely on her own and left to fend for herself.

Impact of War

Phillis struggled to make a life for herself, but food and shelter during the war were both costly and in short supply. Even though she tried to sell her books to support herself, few people had money to spend.

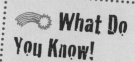

What Do You Know!

Phillis's poem for Washington introduced two phrases that are now commonly used to describe the United States and General Washington. She referred to the land of Columbus as *Columbia*—a description later used to describe the capital: The District of Columbia. Her reference to Washington as "first in place and honours" was misprinted as "first in peace," which is now a favorite description of him.

COLONIAL VIEWS OF SLAVERY In spite of Phillis's fame as a celebrated poet among literary people, many colonists still viewed her as an African slave. Phillis knew what it meant to be a slave—even though one with privileges—and she could remember being free as a young girl in West Africa. It was hard for her to understand how Americans could value their own freedom from the British and still support slavery in the colonies.

During that time, Americans were puzzled by Africans and viewed them as a "different species of man." Consequently, they associated African slaves only with manual labor and considered them inferior to white people. They also depended on slavery to make a living on the frontier. It was one thing to talk about a celebrated African slave poet. It was another thing entirely to buy a book from her.

A Difficult Marriage

On April 1, 1778, Phillis married John Peters, a free black man with big plans. Historical records show him listed as having practiced law, kept a grocery store, and been a baker, a barber, and a bar owner. He was "a man of very handsome person and manners," who was also described as "shiftless [lazy], arrogant, and proud." Whether he was a smart businessman or not, he was a black man during a time that valued only his ability to do manual labor. He could not compete with white men during the tough war times in the colonies.

Writing in Poverty

Phillis and her husband moved to Wilmington, Massachusetts, so that Peters could avoid having to fight in the Revolutionary War. Although the couple lived in poverty, she continued to write. On July 15, 1778, she sent a poem called "On the Death of General Wooster" to General Wooster's wife. Wooster had helped Phillis sell some of her books in the past. He died in a battle against the British, and Phillis wrote the poem to comfort the general's wife. Phillis also continued to write about freedom.

In 1779, she advertised in the *Boston Evening Post* and the *General Advertiser*, in hopes of finding a publisher for a volume of 33 poems and 13 letters. However, the economy after the Revolutionary War was still struggling, and this volume was never published.

Between 1779 and 1783, Phillis and her husband had two children. Phillis worked as a **scullery maid**, and Peters drifted further into debt. He often left Phillis to fend for herself and the children, while he dodged creditors and tried to find work. By 1783, both children had died.

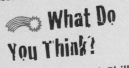

What Do You Think?

Why do you think Phillis wrote an elegy about the death of a baby?

Final Poems

In early 1784, Peters moved Phillis, now pregnant with a third child, into a boarding house in a rundown section of Boston. In February, Phillis wrote a poem honoring the peace treaty signed a few months earlier between the United States and Britain. The poem was called "Liberty and Peace." A short time later, Phillis wrote a poem that she hoped would be included in her second book. The poem memorialized the death of an unknown couple's infant son.

Heartbreak

In early December, one of Susannah Wheatley's relatives found Phillis abandoned, sick, and destitute in the boarding house. "Two of her children were dead, and the third was sick unto death. She was herself suffering . . . reduced to a condition too [hateful] to describe . . . in a filthy apartment . . . , lay dying the mother and the [dying] child. The woman who had stood honored and respected . . . was numbering the last hours of life in a state of the most [complete] misery, surrounded by . . . [wretched] poverty."

On December 5, 1784, at the age of 30, Phillis Wheatley died while her husband was in jail. Her infant son died a few hours later and they were buried together.

Lost Works

After Phillis's death, according to historians, John Peters contacted a woman who had helped Phillis before she died and demanded the manuscripts of the proposed second volume. Sadly, these manuscripts disappeared with Peters and have never been recovered.

Phillis Wheatley and her infant son were buried in Copp's Hill Burial Ground in Boston.

An Important Legacy from a Life of Opposites

Phillis Wheatley thrived while she was a slave, writing about important issues—freedom, religion, and patriotism—during America's revolutionary period. Yet when she was freed from slavery, she died from the burdens of being a free African in a time that did not accept her.

If Phillis Wheatley stood for anything, it was the belief that all people—enslaved, free, black, white, male, female, formally educated or not—could be equal in possessing intelligence and culture. Her life is a reminder of how this belief began to take root during a critical time in America's history. The poetry she left behind, which brilliantly and sensitively spoke to America's growing pains, is her **legacy**.

GLOSSARY

abolition to end or make illegal, especially slavery

abolitionist someone who wants to end slavery

allegiance loyalty to one's nation

alliance an agreement under which two countries agree to help each other, especially militarily

benefactor one who supports causes with money; one who supports artists, musicians, writers, etc.

broadside a large, single-page printed paper

cargo goods that are being transported

chronic asthma a lung condition which continually causes shortness of breath, weezing

civic having to do with a city or citizenship

colonies settlements governed by a mother country, usually overseas

consolation something that offers comfort in a time of grief or suffering

contradiction statements or ideas that are opposite to one another

descent line of ancestry

devastated overwhelmed by emotion, generally sadness

domestic having to do with the home or family

dysentery an intestinal disease causing diarrhea and bloody stool

elegy a poem, usually expressing sadness over a death; consists of three parts: the lament, or expression of grief; an expression of praise for the dead; and a section of comforting words

fugitive one who has run away, especially a slave or refugee

heroic couplet two rhyming lines of poetry in iambic pentameter (a special rhythm of five alternating unstressed and stressed syllables)

idealized something considered as it is desired to be rather than as it actually is

independence being free from outside control or interference

inflammation swelling; a body response sending more blood than usual to an area

influential having lots of influence or power

lament a song or poem expressing grief or sorrow

legacy the impact an individual leaves behind

Loyalist (American Revolution) one who wanted the colonies to remain part of Great Britain; one who stayed loyal to Britain

merchant someone who buys or sells goods for profit

Muslim someone who practices the religion of Islam

natural resources a usable good from nature; for example: timber, water, coal

nomadic moving from place to place; not having a fixed home

oppression the unfair or mean use of authority

Patriot (American Revolution) one who wanted independence for the colonies from Great Britain

patriotic being loyal to one's country

patronage money given, usually by a wealthy individual, to support an artist or writer

personal salvation a Christian belief which emphasizes an individual's need to be saved from sin

plantation a large estate supported by agriculture, especially in the American South; often supported by slave labor

pounds sterling British currency or money

preacher a Christian minister; one who gives sermons

radical one whose beliefs are far from the usual or different from the majority of society

rebuff to refuse or reject

repeal to cancel out a law

respiratory having to do with the lungs

salvation being saved; in religious belief, often entering heaven after death

schooner a ship with two masts, used for sailing along coasts and fishing

scullery maid a female servant who worked in the kitchens; the lowest position for a servant

scurvy a disease caused by not getting enough vitamin C; causes spongy gums and bleeding

[sic] an symbol to indicate that a mistake is originally in the writing; used in books to show that a writer is reproducing the original exactly

spokesperson one who speaks for a group or organization

stature intellectual or moral greatness

subscribe to sign up and pay for a book or magazine

tailor someone who makes or alters clothes

terminally ill suffering from an illness or disease which will probably kill the sufferer

translation a writing which takes a work in one language and puts it in another language

trifle something not very valuable

tumultuous likely to be confusing or disastrous

untainted pure; not dirty

wheezing to breath with difficulty, often with a whistling noise

wretched pitiful; very unhappy

TIMELINE

c. 1754		A girl who will grow up to be Phillis Wheatley is born in West Africa
1761		The girl, at age 7, is kidnapped by slave traders and sold to a wealthy Boston family, who name her Phillis Wheatley
1762		By age 8, Phillis learns to speak, read, and write English
1763–1765		By age 11, Phillis writes about the violence in Boston
1765	*March 27*	The British government imposes the Stamp Act on American colonists
1766–1767		By age 13, Phillis's first poem, "On Messrs Hussey and Coffin" is printed in a newspaper
1770	*March 5*	The Boston Massacre
		Phillis writes a poem about the death of a boy who is accidentally shot during the violence in Boston
1772	*October 8*	A powerful group of Boston's most important citizens test Phillis's intelligence and confirm her work as her own
1773	*May*	Phillis travels to London, where she is celebrated as a literary genius
	September	Phillis abruptly returns to Boston to care for the ailing Mrs. Wheatley; Phillis's book, *Poems on Various Subjects, Religious and Moral* is published. The Wheatleys release Phillis from slavery
1774	*March 3*	Susanna Wheatley dies
	March	Britain imposes the Intolerable Acts on America
	September 5	The Continental Congress meets for the first time
1775	*April 19*	Revolutionary War begins
	June 15	George Washington becomes commander in chief of the colonial forces
	October 26	Phillis writes a patriotic poem honoring George Washington
1776	*March 17*	Phillis meets with George Washington in Boston
	July 4	The Continental Congress creates the Declaration of Independence
1778		The Wheatleys move away. Phillis becomes homeless. Phillis marries John Peters and falls into poverty
1781	*October 18*	British troops surrender to the Continental Army at Yorktown, Virginia
1783		John Peters abandons Phillis, and two of their three children die young; Phillis continues to write while working as a maid
	September 3	Treaty of Paris is signed; American Revolution ends
1784	*February*	Phillis writes her last poems, one of them mourns the death of an infant
	December 5	Phillis dies alone, poor, and sick; her third child dies hours later

FURTHER READING AND WEBSITES

Books

101 Great American Poems. American Poetry & Literacy Project, Dover Publications, 1998.

Alfred F. Young, ed. *Beyond the American Revolution: Explorations in the History of American Radicalism,* Northern Illinois University Press, 1993.

Aloian, Molly. *George Washington: Hero of the American Revolution.* Crabtree Publishing Company, 2013.

Clarke, Gordon. *Significant Battles of the American Revolution.* Crabtree Publishing Company, 2013.

Cocca, Lisa Colozza. *Marquis de Lafayette: Fighting for America's Freedom.* Crabtree Publishing Company, 2013.

Doak, Robin S. *Phillis Wheatley: Slave and Poet* (Signature Lives). Compass Point Books, 2006.

Gary B. Nash, *Race and Revolution,* 1990.

Hudson, Wade. *Pass It On: African-American Poetry for Children.* Scholastic, 1993.

Ira Berlin and Ronald Hoffman, eds., *Slavery and Freedom in the American Revolution,* University of Illinois Press, 1983.

Mason, Helen. *Life on the Homefront during the American Revolution.* Crabtree Publishing Company, 2013.

Perritano, John. *The Causes of the American Revolution.* Crabtree Publishing Company, 2013.

Perritano, John. *The Outcome of the American Revolution.* Crabtree Publishing Company, 2013.

Roberts, Steve. *King George III: England's Struggle to Keep America.* Crabtree Publishing Company, 2013.

Ronald Hoffman and Peter J. Albert, eds., *Women in the Age of the American Revolution,* United States Capitol Historical Society, 1989.

Ronald Hoffman, Thad W. Tate, and Peter J. Albert, eds., *An Uncivil War: The Southern Backcountry during the American Revolution,* United States Capitol Historical Society, 1985.

Sherro, Victoria. *Phillis Wheatley* (Junior World Biographies). Chelsea House Publishers, 1992.

Websites

Phillis Wheatley: The Poetry Foundation.
http://www.poetryfoundation.org/bio/phillis-wheatley

Poems of the American Revolution.
http://www.poets.org/viewmedia.php/prmMID/20281

Poems on various subjects, religious and moral, University of South Carolina, Irvin Department of Rare Books and Special Collections.
http://digital.tcl.sc.edu/cdm/ref/collection/pwp/id/138

The Phillis Wheatley Association.
http://www.philliswheatley.org/

Wheatley Biography.
http://www.vcu.edu/engweb/webtexts/Wheatley/philbio.htm

BIBLIOGRAPHY

Books

Alfred F. Young, ed. *Beyond the American Revolution: Explorations in the History of American Radicalis*m, 1993.

Blair, Margaret. Whitman. *Liberty or Death.* National Geographic Society, 2010.

Carretta, Vincent. *Phillis Wheatley: Biography of a Genius in Bondage.* University of Georgia Press, 2011.

Davenport, John. *The American Revolution.* Thomson Gale Publishing, 2007.

Doak, Robin S. *Phillis Wheatley: Slave and Poet* (Signature Lives). Compass Point Books, 2006.

Gary B. Nash, *Race and Revolution,* 1990.

Ira Berlin and Ronald Hoffman, eds., *Slavery and Freedom in the American Revolution,* 1983.

Mason, Julian D., Jr., ed. *The Poems of Phillis Wheatley.* University of North Carolina Press, 1989.

Ronald Hoffman and Peter J. Albert, eds., *Women in the Age of the American Revolution,* 1989.

Ronald Hoffman, Thad W. Tate, and Peter J. Albert, eds., *An Uncivil War: The Southern Backcountry during the American Revolution,* 1985.

Sherro, Victoria. *Phillis Wheatley* (Junior World Biographies). Chelsea House Publishers, 1992.

Shields, John, ed. *The Collected Works of Phillis Wheatley.* Oxford University Press, 1988.

Wheatley, Phillis. Poems on various subjects, religious and moral. A. Bell, Bookseller, 1773.

Websites

A Celebration of Women Writers. University of Pennsylvania Library.
http://digital.library.upenn.edu/women/ wheatley/liberty/liberty.html

Benjamin Franklin .
http://www.pbs.org/benfranklin/l3_citizen _abolitionist.html

Boston history.
http://www.bostonhistory.org/?s=osh

Colonial Poets.
http://www.poets.org/viewmedia.php/prm MID/5778

Colonial Slave Ships.
http://www.melfisher.org/exhibitions/lasts laveships/slaveships.htm

Colonial Slave Trade.
http://www.medfordhistorical.org/slavetra deletters.php

Colonial Williamsburg Official History Site.
http://www.history.org/

George Whitefield: Great Awakening.
http://greatawakeningdocumentary.com/ exhibits/show/biographies/george- whitefield

Independence Day: A Poetic Voice of the Revolution.
http://womensvoicesforchange.org/tag/ phillis-wheatley

Phillis Wheatley: Old South.
http://www.oldsouth.org/podcasts/aug-18- 1771-phillis

Phillis Wheatley: The Poetry Foundation.
http://www.poetryfoundation.org/bio/ phillis-wheatley

Phillis Wheatley: Women in History.
http://www.historycentral.c.om/NN/
Americans/Women.html

Poems by Phillis Wheatley. "On Being Brought
From Africa to America."
http://www.vcu.edu/engweb/webtexts/
Wheatley/phil.htm

Poems of the American Revolution.
http://www.poets.org/viewmedia.php/prm
MID/20281

Poems on various subjects, religious and moral,
University of South Carolina, Irvin
Department of Rare Books and Special
Collections.
http://digital.tcl.sc.edu/cdm/ref/collection/
pwp/id/138

Quill Pens.
http://www.nhhistory.org/edu/support/
nhgrowingup/quillpens.pdf

The Massachusetts Historical Society.
https://www.masshist.org/endofslavery/
index.cfm?queryID=57

The Phillis Wheatley Association.
http://www.philliswheatley.org/

Today in History: September 1. Library of
Congress.
http://mcmory.loc.gov/ammem/today/
sep01.html

Wheatley Biography.
http://www.vcu.edu/engweb/webtexts/
Wheatley/philbio.htm

INDEX